GODS & GODDESSES
OF THE ANCIENT WORLD

Sobek

BY VIRGINIA LOH-HAGAN

Gods and goddesses were the main characters of myths. Myths are traditional stories from ancient cultures. Storytellers answered questions about the world by creating exciting explanations. People thought myths were true. Myths explained the unexplainable. They helped people make sense of human behavior and nature. Today, we use science to explain the world. But people still love myths. Myths may not be literally true. But they have meaning. They tell us something about our history and culture.

45th Parallel Press

Published in the United States of America by Cherry Lake Publishing
Ann Arbor, Michigan
www.cherrylakepublishing.com

Reading Adviser: Marla Conn, MS, Ed., Literacy specialist, Read-Ability, Inc.
Book Design: Jen Wahi

Photo Credits: ©Howard David Johnson, 2019, cover, 1, 12; ©Julian W/Shutterstock, 5; ©Anton_Ivanov/Shutterstock, 6;
©Supermop/Shutterstock, 9; ©bastetamon/Shutterstock, 11; ©IgorZh/Shutterstock, 15; ©Natalia Golovina/Shutterstock, 17;
Leon Jean Joseph Dubois (1780–1846)/rawpixel/Public domain, 19; ©Smeade/Shutterstock, 21; ©Certe/Shutterstock, 22;
©ChameleonsEye/Shutterstock, 25; ©Filipe.Lopes/Shutterstock, 26; ©Blue Ice/Shutterstock, 29

45th Parallel Press is an imprint of Cherry Lake Publishing.

Library of Congress Cataloging-in-Publication Data

Names: Loh-Hagan, Virginia, author. | Loh-Hagan, Virginia. Gods & goddesses of the ancient world.
Title: Sobek / written by Virginia Loh-Hagan.
Description: Ann Arbor, Michigan : Cherry Lake Publishing, 2019. | Series: Gods and goddesses of the ancient world
Identifiers: LCCN 2019004187 | ISBN 9781534147775 (hardcover) | ISBN 9781534149205 (pdf) | ISBN 9781534150638 (pbk.) |
    ISBN 9781534152069 (hosted ebook)
Subjects: LCSH: Sobek (Egyptian deity)—Juvenile literature. | Gods, Egyptian—Juvenile literature. | Mythology, Egyptian—
    Juvenile literature.
Classification: LCC BL2450.S68 L64 2019 | DDC 299/.312113—dc23
LC record available at https://lccn.loc.gov/2019004187

Printed in the United States of America
Corporate Graphics

ABOUT THE AUTHOR:

Dr. Virginia Loh-Hagan is an author, university professor, former classroom teacher, and curriculum designer. She's scared of crocodiles. She lives in San Diego with her very tall husband and very naughty dogs. To learn more about her, visit www.virginialoh.com.

TABLE OF CONTENTS

ABOUT THE AUTHOR 2

CHAPTER 1:
CROCODILE KING 4

CHAPTER 2:
BEWARE OF CROCODILES! 8

CHAPTER 3:
A NEST OF CROCODILES 14

CHAPTER 4:
CREATOR GOD 20

CHAPTER 5:
SAVED BY A CROCODILE 24

DID YOU KNOW? 30
CONSIDER THIS! 31
LEARN MORE 31
GLOSSARY 32
INDEX 32

CROCODILE KING

Who is Sobek? What does he look like?

Sobek was an **ancient** Egyptian god. Ancient means old. Egypt is a country in the Middle East. It's in North Africa.

Sobek was the god of crocodiles. He lived in the Nile River. Ancient Egyptians depended on the Nile River. Egypt doesn't get much rain. But the Nile River **flooded**. Flooding is when water spills over. The flooding left behind black **silt**. Silt is rich soil. This silt made the land **fertile**. Fertile means capable of growing food.

Ancient Egyptians worshipped the Nile River. But they also feared it. A high flood destroyed cities. A low flood meant people couldn't grow food. And crocodiles lived in the Nile. They killed people. Sobek protected people from crocodiles.

Sobek worked with Hapi. Hapi was the god of the Nile River. He was the god of its annual flooding. Annual means happening every year.

Nile crocodiles have the strongest bite in the animal kingdom.

Crocodiles were known to serve Hapi.

Sobek was big. He had a man's body. He had a crocodile's head. Sometimes, he took the crocodile's whole form. Sometimes, he had a crocodile's body. He had a falcon's head. He wore a double crown.

He wore a **headdress**. A headdress is a head covering. It's like a crown. Sobek wore feathers in his headdress.

He wore a sun **disc**. Discs are flat circles. Sobek held a **scepter**. Scepters are long poles. They represent power.

Family Tree

Great-grandparents: Shu (god of light and dry air) and Tefnut (goddess of wet air and rain)

Grandparents: Geb (god of the earth) and Nut (goddess of the sky)

Parents: Set (god of disorder and deserts) and Neith (goddess of war, hunting, and wisdom)

Wife: Renenutet (goddess of plenty and good fortune) or Meskhenet (goddess of childbirth) or Hathor (goddess of motherhood) or Heqet (goddess of fertility) or Taweret (goddess of childbirth)

Children: Khonsu (god of moon and time) or Khnum (god of the source of the Nile)

CHAPTER 2

BEWARE OF CROCODILES!

What is Sobek's personality like? What are Sobek's powers? What does he do?

Like Nile crocodiles, Sobek was violent. He was fierce. He was a fighter. He had a strong bite. He was called "pointed of teeth." But Nile crocodiles were also known to be good parents. They cared for their babies. They carried babies in their mouths. They protected their babies. So, Sobek was also a protector god.

The Nile River had many dangers. Ancient Egyptians worked and lived around the Nile. They worshipped and feared crocodiles. They prayed to Sobek. They gave him gifts. They threw him parties. Sobek kept people safe from crocodiles. He controlled the crocodiles. He healed people. He warded off evil.

Nile crocodiles guard their nests.

All in the Family

Geb was the god of earth. Earth was called the "house of Geb." The royal throne was called the "throne of Geb." Geb was a member of the Great Ennead. The Ennead were the 9 most important gods and goddesses. They were the original gods and goddesses. Geb was mostly in a man's form. Sometimes, he had a snake's head. Sometimes, he had a goose's head. He had a beard. His laugh created earthquakes. He helped crops grow. He opened his mouth and set the dead free from their tombs. Geb and Nut were twins. Nut was the goddess of the sky. Geb and Nut were born at the same time. They held tightly to each other's arms. Their father had to separate them. This is why the earth and sky are separated by air. As a goose, Geb was thought to have laid a special egg. This is the egg that created the world.

 In early stories, Sobek was an evil god. Then, he turned into a good god.

Ancient Egyptians believed in the **afterlife**. Afterlife is the life after death. Ancient Egyptians made **mummies**. Mummies were dried out dead bodies. Ancient Egyptians wrapped the bodies. This process kept bodies from rotting. They believed it let souls move into another world.

Ancient Egyptians also made crocodile mummies. They did this to honor Sobek. They put the crocodile mummies with the people mummies. They wanted Sobek's protection in the afterlife. Sobek helped dead souls. He gave them back their sight. He gave them back their senses.

Nile crocodiles have many babies. They lay 10 to 100 eggs. Because of this, Sobek was a fertility god. He's called the "lord of the waters." He helped control the waters. He helped make the silt. He made the plants grow. He made all the animals. There are many animals in the Nile River.

Nile crocodiles are powerful. They are fast. They awe people with their strength. As such, Sobek was a symbol of power. He protected **pharaohs**. Pharaohs were ancient Egyptian rulers. Sobek gave pharaohs courage. He helped them overcome problems. He helped them win wars. He protected the Egyptian army.

 Sobek said, "I will eat with my mouth. I will pee. I will make babies."

CHAPTER 3

A NEST OF CROCODILES

Who are Sobek's parents? Who are his wives? Who are his children?

There's not much known about how Sobek was born. In some stories, Sobek's father was Set. Set was the god of storms. He was the god of **chaos**. Chaos means disorder. Sobek's mother was Neith. She was the goddess of war. She was the goddess of hunting. She was the goddess of wisdom. She was the goddess of weaving. She weaved the world's events. She did this each day.

In some stories, Neith was a water goddess. Set may have made a storm. He and Neith had Sobek. Neith was also known as the Nurse of Crocodiles.

 When Sobek was born, he was called the Rager.

Real World Connection

In ancient times, crocodiles basked in the sun around Kom Ombo. Kom Ombo means the "hill of gold." It's a city in Egypt. It's close to the Nile River. It has a temple. The temple is dedicated to Sobek and Horus the Elder. Today, there's a Crocodile Museum. It's Egypt's first museum devoted to crocodiles. It started in 2012. It has a collection of crocodile mummies. The mummies are of different sizes. Some mummies had gold and ivory teeth and eyes. Ancient Egyptians put the gems in the mummies. The crocodile mummies are placed on a sand hill. They look like they're lying on the banks of the Nile River. Banks are the land on the side of rivers. Visitors can see how crocodiles spent their time in ancient Egypt. The museum also has crocodile eggs and babies. It has statues of Sobek. Before it was a museum, the building was a police station.

In most stories, Sobek was married to Renenutet. Renenutet was the goddess of **harvest**. Harvest is the gathering of crops. Renenutet had a snake's head. She cared for others.

There may have been other wives. Meskhenet was the goddess of childbirth. She breathed a soul into each child. Hathor was the goddess of motherhood. She had a cow's head. Tawaret was the goddess of childbirth. She was a hippo. She had the back of a crocodile. She protected women as they gave birth.

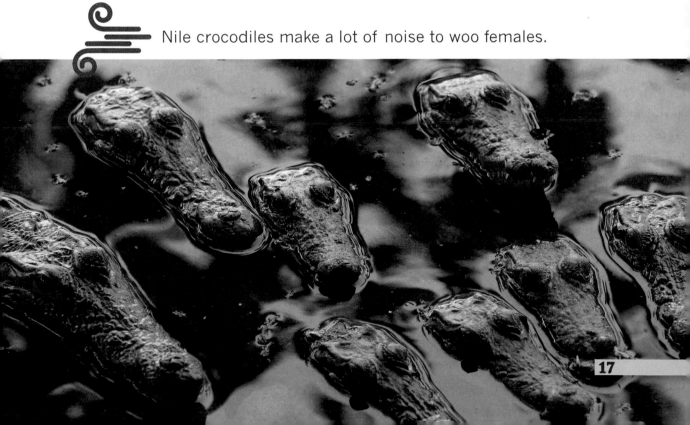

Nile crocodiles make a lot of noise to woo females.

In some stories, Sobek had 2 sons. Their names were Khnum and Khonsu.

Khnum was a water god. He had a crocodile's head. He was the god of the source of the Nile. He controlled the amount of silt in the Nile. He took some silt. He put it on a potter's wheel. This is how he made human bodies.

Khonsu's name means "traveler." He was the god of the moon. Every night, he traveled across the night sky. He watched over those who traveled at night. He protected against wild animals. Some nights, he made the moon shine brighter. This caused females to be fertile. Khonsu was also the god of time.

 Khonsu is typically shown with a moon disc above his head.

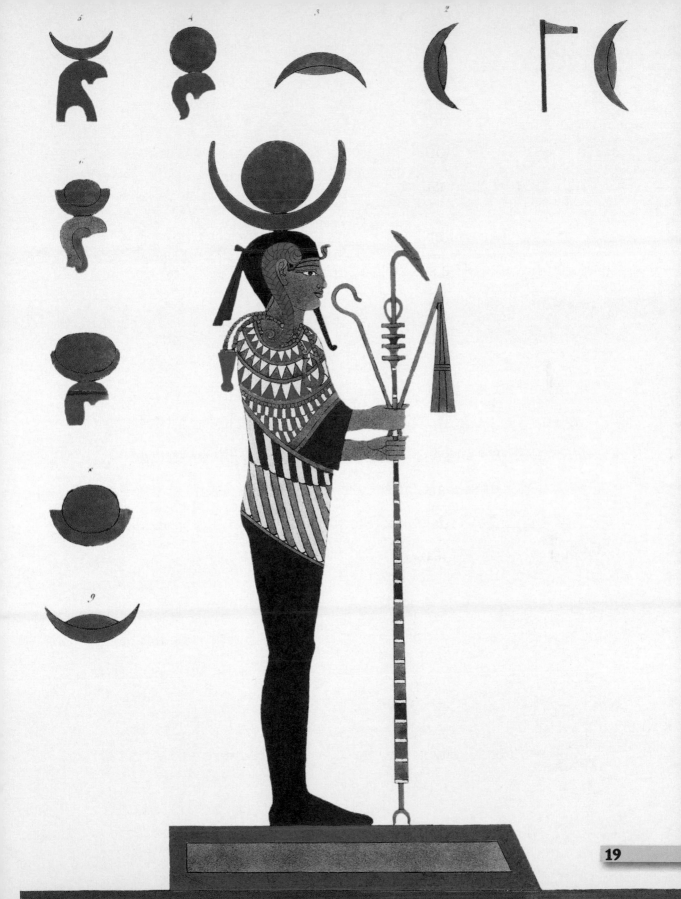

CHAPTER 4

CREATOR GOD

How does Sobek create the world? How does he create the Nile River? How does he act like crocodiles?

In some stories, Sobek was a **creator god**. Creator gods made the world.

Nun was the first waters. He was the water of chaos. Before Sobek, the world was crazy. Nun's waters were dangerous. They were swirling with frogs and crocodiles. Out of these waters, a mound of dirt emerged. This mound was shaped like an egg. Sunlight hit the mound. It gave the dirt power. The dirt became Sobek.

As a crocodile, Sobek was connected to the sun. Crocodiles seem to follow the sun's movement. They spend the night in water. They come out when the sun shines. They lay in the sun all day long.

Sobek was linked to Ra. Ra was the Sun God. Sometimes, Sobek was called Sobek-Ra.

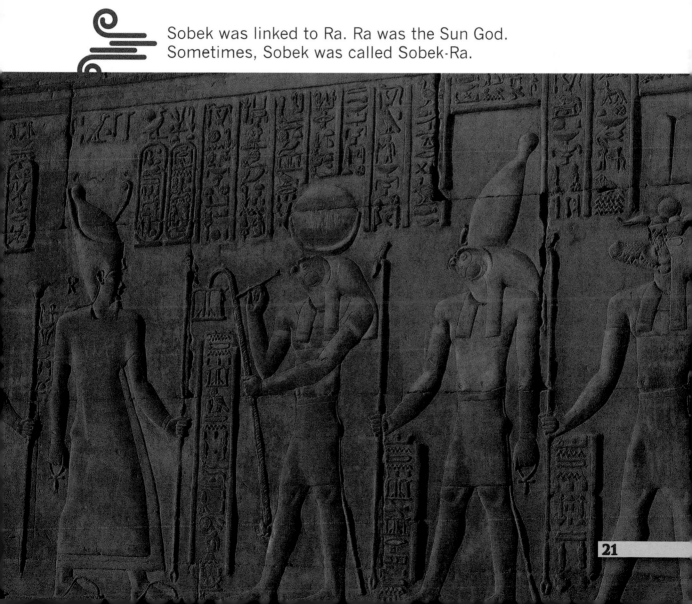

Sobek was linked to Hapi.

It took a lot of energy to be born. When he emerged, he sweated. His sweat became the Nile River.

Sobek was very fertile. So, he laid many eggs. As a crocodile, Sobek knew exactly where to lay eggs. Crocodiles can sense the height of floods. They build their nests high. They build them above flood level.

Sobek's eggs became things. They made plants. They made mountains. They made seasons. They made humans.

Cross-Cultural Connection

The River Ganges flows through India and Bangladesh. It's thought to be a holy river. Ganga was a river goddess. She was beautiful. She wore a white crown. She had 4 arms. She held a water lily, water pot, holy beads, and a lute. Lutes are like guitars. Ganga sat on a throne. She was surrounded by crocodiles. She rode Makara. Makara had a land animal's head. Makara had sea animal's tail. Sometimes, Makara was a crocodile. Ganga was created from the sweat of a powerful god. At first, Ganga lived in heaven. She was devoted to Lord Krishna. Lord Krishna's lover got jealous. She cursed Ganga. She threw her down to earth. Ganga hit the earth. She became a flowing river. She became the River Ganges. People celebrate the river coming to earth. They wash themselves in the river. They pray to Ganga. They thought the water cleaned them of sins.

CHAPTER 5

SAVED BY A CROCODILE

What are some stories about Sobek? How is he helpful?
How is he not helpful?

There are several stories about Sobek. He's most famous
for helping Isis. Isis and Osiris were powerful gods. They
got married. They ruled the world. Set was jealous. He
wanted power. He tricked Osiris. He made Osiris get into
a **coffin**. Coffins are cases that hold dead bodies. He threw
the coffin into the Nile River.

Isis, Hapi, and Sobek are all connected to the flooding
of the Nile River.

Isis was sad. She searched for Osiris. She cried many tears. She flooded the river. She found the coffin with Osiris. She brought him back to life. Set found out. He hacked Osiris's body into many pieces. He threw them in the Nile.

Sobek searched the Nile. He helped find Osiris's body parts. He carried them to the side of the river. He made sure the body parts were safe. This made Sobek the protector of **divine** rulers. Divine means godly.

In another version, Sobek was not helpful. He was really hungry. He didn't save Osiris's body parts. He ate them instead. The gods got mad at him. They punished him. They cut off his tongue. This is how ancient Egyptians explained why crocodiles don't have tongues. Crocodile tongues are attached to the roofs of their mouths. They don't move.

Sobek helped Isis in another story. Isis had a son. Her son was Horus. She needed to protect him from Set. She hid him

 Alligators have tongues. Crocodiles do not.

Explained By Science

Nile crocodiles are large reptiles. They're Africa's largest freshwater predator. Predators are hunters. Nile crocodiles are about 20 feet (6 meters) long. They weigh up to 1,650 pounds (748 kilograms). They live around the Nile River. They mainly eat fish. But they attack anything in their path. They eat zebras, small hippos, and other crocodiles. They're even known to eat humans. About 200 people die each year from a Nile crocodile attack. Nile crocodiles are very violent. They wait for their prey. They can wait for weeks. They wait for the right moment to attack. They have special senses on their scaly skin. These senses track movements in water. They have special blood. Their blood lets them sit still in water for up to 2 hours. They have a powerful bite. Their sharp teeth sink into meat. Their strong jaws take grip. Nothing can get loose. Nile crocodiles apply a lot of force. They hold down their prey.

Sobek became linked with the most powerful Egyptian gods.

by the Nile River. Sobek helped protect him. When Horus grew up, he fought Set. Horus and Set fought for 80 years. Sobek helped Horus. But Sobek also helped Set. When Set lost, his army turned into crocodiles. Sobek helped Set's army escape Horus.

Don't anger the gods. Sobek had great powers. And he knew how to use them.

DID YOU KNOW?

- Sobek was called the Lord of the Faiyum. Faiyum is a city in Egypt. It was called Crocodile City. A pet crocodile was kept in a special lake. It was worshipped. It was called the "son of Sobek." It was fed good cuts of meat. It was fed milk mixed with honey. It was decorated with gems. When it died, it was mummified. A new pet crocodile took its place.

- Herodotus was an ancient Greek historian. He wrote that any person killed by a crocodile in Faiyum was thought to be divine. These people were given special ceremonies. They were buried in special coffins.

- Amenemhat III was a pharaoh. He ruled around 1860 BCE. He built a pyramid in Faiyum. He said he was "beloved of Sobek." He promoted Sobek. He treated him like Horus. This made Sobek more important to pharaohs.

- Sobek's priests were called "prophets of the crocodile gods." Prophets are people who speak for the gods. They're also teachers of gods.

- Sobekneferu was a pharaoh. She ruled after the death of her brother. She ruled from 1806 to 1802 BCE. Her name means the "beauty of Sobek." She's the first known female pharaoh.

- Sobek had some temples. Temples are places of worship. They're like churches. Most of Sobek's temples were in parts of Egypt where crocodiles were common.

- Ancient Egyptians tried to feed crocodiles. This meant they were blessed by Sobek.

- Sobekhotep was a popular ancient Egyptian name. It means "Sobek is pleased."

CONSIDER THIS!

TAKE A POSITION! Read the 45th Parallel Press about Hapi. How are Hapi and Sobek connected? Which god is more important? Argue your point with reasons and evidence.

SAY WHAT? Some people confuse crocodiles and alligators. Learn more about crocodiles. Learn more about alligators. Explain how they're the same. Explain how they're different. How can you tell alligators and crocodiles apart?

THINK ABOUT IT! Many ancient Egyptian gods had animal heads. Which animal head would you choose? Why? What would it symbolize?

LEARN MORE

Braun, Eric. *Egyptian Myths*. North Mankato, MN: Capstone Press, 2019.

Napoli, Donna Jo, and Christina Balit (illust.). *Treasury of Egyptian Mythology: Classic Stories of Gods, Goddesses, Monsters, and Mortals*. Washington, DC: National Geographic Kids, 2013.

Reinhart, Matthew, and Robert Sabuda. *Gods and Heroes*. Somerville, MA: Candlewick Press, 2010.

GLOSSARY

afterlife (AF-tur-life) life after death

ancient (AYN-shuhnt) old, from a long time ago

chaos (KAY-ahs) disorder

coffin (KAW-fin) a case that holds a dead body

creator god (kree-AY-tur GAHD) a god who creates the world

disc (DISK) flat circle

divine (dih-VINE) godly

fertile (FUR-tuhl) the ability to grow more food or make more babies

flooded (FLUHD-id) water spilling over on to the land

harvest (HAHR-vist) the gathering of crops

headdress (HED-dres) a fancy head covering like a crown

mummies (MUHM-eez) wrapped bodies used as part of the embalming process

pharaohs (FAIR-ohz) ancient Egyptian rulers

scepter (SEP-tur) a long pole used to represent power

silt (SILT) rich soil

INDEX

A
afterlife, 11

C
crocodiles, 4–6, 8–9, 11, 13, 15–18, 21–22, 27, 30

E
Egypt, 4

G
Geb, 7, 10

H
Hapi, 5, 22, 24
Horus, 28–29

I
Isis, 24, 27–29

N
Nile River, 4–5, 8–9, 13, 18, 22, 24–25, 27, 29
Nut, 7, 10

O
Osiris, 24, 27

R
Ra, 21

S
Set, 7, 14–15, 24, 28–29
Sobek, 30
   as creator god, 20–22
   family, 7, 14–19
   parents, 7, 14–15
   personality, 8
   stories about, 24–29
   what he did, 8–9, 13
   what he looked like, 6–7
   who he is, 4–7
   wives, 7, 17